Praise for *The Poetry of History*

"Jeff Rimland intricately weaves history through his gift of beautifully written poetry, in a way that will make the reader both ponder and reflect on the people and events who have changed the course of history for better or for worse.

"Eloquently written, Jeff Rimland gives us a look into some of the most historic events in history from 1014 AD to modern day. The Poetry of History is an illustrated compilation of thirty-one short, well-researched historical facts which are accompanied by a reflective poem. In "Mason Dixon Line" we learn about the 1863 Battle of Gettysburg while we contemplate how we often take the sacrifices from the past for granted. In "The Last Good War" history buffs will love reading about World War II. In "Rosa" and "Amelia" we reflect on two women who have paved the way for women's advancements and racial equality. From presidents, to tsunamis, to generals, bombings, bloodshed and discoveries, The Poetry of History has it all. Jeff Rimland has encompassed the history of the world in one concise, easy-to-read book which will have readers coming back for more."

Kerriann Flanagan Brosky, Author and Historian

"It is fascinating to watch which aspects of history are singled out by Jeff Rimland. He creates both a personal and poetic overview of our history. By casting facts (and pictures) into a personal perspective, he not only serves as our teacher, but he gifts us a personal legacy."

Dr. David B. Axelrod, Fulbright and Poet Laureate

"The Poetry of History by Jeff Rimland takes us on a journey that is both educational and entertaining. Each epic historical event is complemented with unique poetry. It can be read chronologically or randomly without losing impact. Warning: Whatever page you choose, you'll be tempted to turn to the next. Riveting work is testament to a seasoned author. Read and enjoy."

Ron Scott, Nassau County Poet Laureate Society

THE
POETRY OF HISTORY

THE
POETRY OF HISTORY

BY

JEFF RIMLAND

Published by: Jeff Rimland

ISBN (paperback) 978-1-7378629-0-1
ISBN (eBook) 978-1-7378629-1-8.

To order additional copies of this book contact the author:
jeffrimland@msn.com

Also by Jeff Rimland:

A Widowers Journey; A Life of Loss and Love
Our Gift to Each Other; Heartfelt Poems of Our Love
Reflections on Half a Century
Knowledge then Wisdom perhaps

TABLE OF CONTENTS

ACKNOWLEDGEMENTS

Special thanks to my friend and fellow author John P. Cardone for the design and layout of the interior pages, his work on the photographs, and his instrumental inspiration and assistance in publishing this book. Also, many thanks to my son, David Rimland, for his work on editing this book, and to my daughter-in-law Angela Rimland for creating the front and back covers. And thank you to David Axelrod for his final edit and review work making the book the best it could be. Finally, thanks to my friend Professor Geoff Salzman for writing the Foreword and meeting with me for coffee as we discussed present and historical events every Sunday morning for the last 20 years.

FOREWORD

Historical writing should reflect the culture of the time and ideas and facts related to that time. Historical writing should also act as a window to understanding the emotions of an event or a time period. Poetry is indeed a medium that acts as a conduit for all these attributes. In this collection of historical poems, Jeff Rimland has painstakingly researched the facts behind each event or historical figure. Only, as an accomplished author could do, he placed each event into a distinct poetic style. By so doing, each event took on a rhythm of its own, thus giving the reader more insight and a better understanding of that event. By reading each poem along with its historical background, you will be able to gain a greater appreciation of the window of time.

Professor Geoff Salzman
Farmingdale State College
State University of New York

INTRODUCTION

This volume of poetry is unique. It contains photographs, descriptions, and poetry of historical figures and events. The photographs and descriptions are authentic, but the poetry is the Author's interpretation and historically accurate.

These events and historical figures are placed in chronological order, going as far back in history as 1014 A.D. They have been chosen according to the Author's individual artistic and historical preferences.

The *Poetry of History* is designed to be read randomly, so feel free to take your time. Enjoy!

Historically yours,

Jeff Rimland

DEDICATION

I dedicate this volume of historical poetry to my children, their life partners, and to my grandchildren, so they continue to learn from history.

And to my parents, Dorothy and Murray Rimland, who taught me a love of history, their history, and now all our history.

1014-2014 Death and Violence

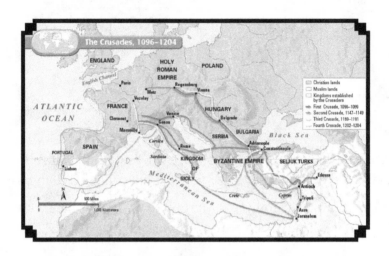

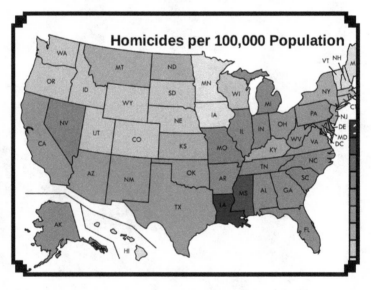

Since 1014 A.D., there has been fighting and death because of the Crusades, empire disputes, World War I, World War II, Korean War, Vietnam War, Terrorism, and continual uprisings and violence by various factions in the Middle East, Turkey, Europe, and in the United States. Many of the places mentioned are all too familiar, where so much death and violence has occurred. Sadly, we have become numb and desensitized.

Death and Violence in All Too Familiar Places

Defending Christians and Muslims crusading and murdering each other
for the one true religion from before and after 1014.
Arabs and Israelis killing each other over land promised since 1927.
Death and Violence in all too familiar places.

The Ottoman Empire, before and after the Great War 1914-1918,
where the Ottoman Turks fought on the side of the Central powers,
still beheading, hand severing, and dismembering as a means of justice.
Death and Violence in all too familiar places.

The British creating boundaries and barriers and countries,
cut out of the Ottoman's kingdoms in Jordan, Egypt, Ukraine, Russia,
Armenia, Bosnia and Herzegovina, Croatia, Persia, Iran, Iraq,
Kosovo, Lebanon, Libya, Romania, Serbia, Somalia, Sudan, Syria,
Turkey, Yemen,
and the list goes on and on.
Death and Violence in all too familiar places.

Pogroms in Belarus, deaths in Poland to Germany, Warsaw to Auschwitz.
Terrorism in Afghanistan to Iraq, ISIL to ISIS to Iran.
Wars we don't start, but ones we finish.
Death and Violence in all too familiar places.

Flight over Lockerbie.
Flight over Seoul.
Flight of MH 17.
Drones over terror groups, and state backed terrorist groups in Pakistan,
Iraq, Syria, Iran.
Death and violence in all too familiar places.

Prior to the Civil War 1854.
Jim Crow South 1954.
Ferguson, Missouri and Police Officers assassinated in Brooklyn, NY in 2014.
Endless battles for equality and justice.
Death in the hundreds and thousands and in threes.

Lord, we need some hope and salvation,
but all we see is
Death and Violence in all too familiar places.

1452 Joan of Arc

Joan of Arc, nicknamed "The Maid of Orléans," is considered a heroine of France for her role during the Hundred Years' War and was canonized as a Saint. She was born to Jacques D'Arc and Isabelle Romée at Domrémy in northeast France. She died at age 19, as she was being burned at the stake by the English.

Joan

God's warrior,
gilded swords and shields.
Old beyond her 15 years,
answering the call to her country,
her kingdom, and her God.
Visions aided her canonization to sainthood,
500 years later.
Burned at the stake by the English,
for her loyalty to France by age 19.

One of the first woman activists,
forged the way forward for women,
to stand up for a cause greater than themselves.

1860 Florence Nightingale

Florence Nightingale was an English social reformer, statistician, and the founder of modern nursing. Nightingale came to prominence while serving as a manager and trainer of nurses during the Crimean War, in which she organized to care for wounded soldiers at Constantinople, Turkey.

Florence Nightingale was born into a wealthy family. Her parents expected her to marry into wealth, but she believed her calling was nursing. The Crimean War was fought between Britain/ France versus Russia, battling for the control of the Ottoman Empire in Turkey. After Florence trained to be a nurse in Germany, the British government requested her service to help save lives in Crimea. Soldiers were dying, not from battle but disease. Florence walked the hospital ward with a lantern checking on her patients nightly, then referred to as "The lady with the lamp."

Based upon a report Nightingale issued, commenting on the casualty level before her service, 16,000 out of 18,000 soldiers died (88% mortality rate) from disease, not battle wounds.

After she administered her service, the mortality rate was only 2%.

Florence

Named after a city in Italy,
made her way through life by caring,
paving the way for modern nursing.
The "lady with the lamp."

Then, no approval by her family,
who thought she should not have a calling.

Taking a 88% mortality rate to a 2% mortality rate!

Talk about a calling; nursing and healing!
She was the epitome of what nursing should be.
Saving lives and teaching,
nursing and creating standards,
that are still used today. `

Now, can you imagine what her parents would have felt
when the history books displayed her achievements!

1863 Battle of Gettysburg

The Battle of Gettysburg was the most significant and bloodiest battle ever fought in North America. In July 1863, the Union Army of the Potomac and the Confederate Army of Northern Virginia turned a small town in Pennsylvania into the site of a struggle for the future of the United States. More than 50,000 men fell as casualties (men listed as killed, wounded, or missing/captured), a scale of suffering never seen before or since on American soil.

According to many historians, Gettysburg was the turning point of the American Civil War. In retrospect, it was the Confederacy's best chance to achieve victory, but to no avail. Ultimately the Battle of Gettysburg breathed new life into the Union war effort.

Mason Dixon Line

Winding through Manassas,
on the way to Appomattox Courthouse,
up through the deadly fields of Gettysburg,
driving my 21st Century hybrid,
gave me pause,
as the traffic was backed up on 15 North.
My biggest problem was making it to the next rest stop.

Reflecting on the beautiful lush green fields,
showing farm houses, and horses,
crossing the river, on a modern bridge,
seeing the sign, "Potomac River,"
gave me pause.

Realizing that as I traveled on black top,
here would lie, 51,112 dead
of Lee's Army of Northern Virginia,
and of Meade's Army of the Potomac
so that the Union could be saved,
so that future generations can travel over that river,
without fear of marching to their death,
or without fear of enslavement,
or without fear of unequal rights of citizenship.

1900-2020 Immigration

In the last 120 years, immigration has changed vastly from the boatloads arriving in ports along the east and west coasts of the United States. From the 1880s to the 1950s, and in the 21st century, immigrants came to the U.S. searching for a better life. The United States government welcomed immigrants into their groups like the Irish, Italians, Jews from Eastern Europe, and presently those from Latin America to build a better life.

Today immigrants are coming to America, but the United States government is not as welcoming, saying, "please do not come here now."

Immigration

Great-Great, Grandparents, entire families,
packing up, walking out, shipping out.
Just their clothes on their backs,
and small tokens of their lives,
wrapped in cheesecloth.

Idealistic visions,
keeping focus on the goal:
The goal of America,
to escape persecution, to build a life.

Ethnic groups being welcomed,
by their own,
by the government.

Back then:
Mulberry Street.
China Town.
Hester Street.
Lower East Side.

San Francisco,
Los Angeles,
Chicago,
Philadelphia.

Now,
Phoenix,
San Antonio,
Guatemala,
El Salvador,
Mexico,
Families.

Immigrants are welcome, but only by their own.
The government says, "please do not come here now."
But now, never seems to come around.

1902 General John J. Pershing

During World War I, U.S. Army General John J. Pershing (1860-1948) commanded the American Expeditionary Force (AEF) in Europe. The president and first captain of the West Point class of 1886, he served in various battles involving the American Indian campaign, Spanish and Philippine-American Wars. Further, he led a punitive raid against the Mexican revolutionary Pancho Villa.

In 1917, President Woodrow Wilson selected Pershing to command the American troops in Europe. Although Pershing aimed to maintain the independence of the AEF, his willingness to integrate into Allied operations helped bring about the armistice with Germany. After the war, Pershing served as army chief of staff from 1921 to 1924.

Ironically, U.S. President Woodrow Wilson had categorized World War I as the "War to end all Wars."

General Pershing

Forty years old in a new century,
brought back memories,
of ages twenty-seven to thirty,
when fighting for the US Cavalry against the Indians:
gave me the experience to fight the next war,
the war to end all wars.

1898 brought me to fight
in the Philippines and Cuba, against the Spanish,
gave me the experience to fight the next war,
the war to end all wars.

Preparing me for 1917,
which gave me the experience to handle
all the death I would see.

From nerve gas to trench warfare,
from the bombings to the shelling and the machine-gun sounds,
of inexplicable horror,
where I would see many of my soldiers dying,
in the war to end all wars.

Gave me the experience to teach my sons,
that war is hell,
but many times necessary
to rid the world of evil.
When leaders assert power over their citizens,
people must fight the oppression.

1903 The Wright Brothers

In 1903 the Wright Brothers were credited with inventing, building, and flying the world's first successful motor-operated Airplane. The brothers were also the first to create aircraft controls that made the fixed-wing powered flight possible.

When Orville and Wilbur Wright went to grade school and secondary school, they studied hard and performed well. During this period, their mother became ill, and Orville and Wilbur cared for her before and after school. Years later, the brothers owned printing and bicycle businesses, but the Airplane remained a focus through the late 1890s and up to 1902. An interesting fact is the "airplane" was initially known as the "aero plane."

Then in 1903, at Kittyhawk, North Carolina, their Airplane safely took off and safely landed.

Flight of the Wright Brothers

Maybe it was soaring in their bedroom,
through the blankets raised high like mountains,
and landing on the mattress runway.
Or perhaps the paper "aero plane"
that Wilbur folded and folded,
might have seemed just magical.

Orville's bicycle with the wheels speeding so fast,
maybe could help a wooden "aero plane"
get off the ground.

The wood and the canvas,
the three-way control,
the trying, trying, and trying.
the redesign, redesign, and redesigning.

Little did the brothers know
that their flight in 1903
would make such a difference in the world.

When growing up, all they knew was reading and studying,
while caring for their mother, and years later,
credited with the invention of the airplane,
and possibly a message from their mother,
much like a "reward" for a job well done.

1918 Spanish Flu

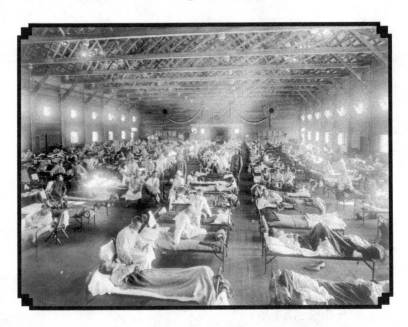

The Spanish influenza epidemic in 1918-1919 claimed the lives of 40 million people worldwide. The virus swept through cities worldwide, and some estimates put total deaths closer to 70 million. Reports described people dying within hours of first feeling ill, and the mortality rate was highest among adults under age 50.

Strangely, victims of the Spanish Flu were identified by having a blue hue to their skin. Further, many soldiers fighting in World War I lived through heavy combat but died instead of the Spanish Flu.

Irony of the Spanish Flu

Fighting across Europe,
running behind tanks,
jumping in trenches.
Dodging bullets, avoiding mustard gas,
twenty-four months at the gates of hell.
Bringing me to the brink of death,
in a military hospital far from home.

Coughing, pale, blue-faced,
hardly able to breathe,
in a military hospital far from home.

I think, what would make me happy,
right about now-
to take my last breath,
with you in my arms.

1915-1920 Marconi and the Crystal Radio

Guglielmo Marconi was an Italian inventor and electrical engineer known for his pioneering work on long-distance radio transmission, Marconi's law, and a radio telegraph system. For many decades the radio was the primary source of entertainment and information—it is still prominent today.

The Center of Her World

Seated on the floor,
with her brother and sister,
her parents shushed them.

When the President had his fireside chat, and Sherlock Holmes
and the other detective shows came on,
and A Wonderful Life was on,
and Frank Sinatra crooned, and
Bob Hope made her laugh.

Even when TV was invented,
she listened in the morning and at night,
after she finished her homework,
or wanted a companion at lunch time,
when she got her first job in NYC,
working at Miller Wohl in 1949.

No doubt this piece of technology influenced her,
to, then in 1967, buy her 13-year-old son,
a transistor radio.

Marconi knew he was enhancing communication,
but probably never thought the crystal radio
would be the center of her world,
growing up in the 1930s and 1940s.

1914-1918 World War I

World War I, ironically known as "The War to end all Wars," where Americans and its Allies fought their hearts out. Then on the 11th day of the 11th Month in 1918, World War I ended, and this date became known as Armistice Day. Then, in 1954, Armistice Day became Veterans Day in the U.S.

In Memoriam

Think about what courage is.

We all show courageous behavior in our lives.
Courage to face the day,
in the midst of life's challenges.
Courage to stand up for what is right and just,
on the job,
in our community.
Courage to lead your parents, children or spouse or relatives or friends
away from despair and into the light of hope.

On this day we see what courage is.
The ultimate courageous act and the ultimate price.
Our military has fought and died,
so we can be free and live our lives,
so we can pay it forward to show our soldiers' souls,
that the price paid was not in vain.

1920 Madame Curie

Madame Marie Curie (1867-1934) was a Polish and French physicist and chemist who conducted early research on radioactivity. As the first of five Nobel Prizes in her family, she was the first woman to win a Nobel Prize, the first person and the only woman to win the Nobel Prize twice, and the only person to win the Nobel Prize in two scientific fields. She was also the first woman to become a professor at the University of Paris in 1906.

Madame

She was radiant.
A shining star amongst women.
Encroaching on a man's territory.
Successful in her field,
with the help of her husband.

She was radiant.
A shining Nobel Prize,
after discovering radiation.
She lived to always prove herself,
and died from her discovery.

1929 The Great Depression and Herbert Hoover

The Great Depression was the worldwide economic collapse following the stock market crash in 1929, in which unemployment remained high for an extended period, and many businesses failed. Bread lines were everyday scenes.

The President of the United States at this time was Herbert Hoover. He was a mining engineer and had traveled to China during the Boxer Rebellion (1900) and assisted in feeding Chinese peasants. Hoover, referred to as "The Great Humanitarian" in his efforts to provide food to thousands in the aftermath of World War 1. Eventually, Herbert Hoover became the head of the Food Administration, where he was responsible for feeding 20 million U.S. citizens. Hoover's policies were often blamed for not solving the many issues involving the Great Depression. Herbert Hoover served as President from 1928 until 1932.

On the Eve

Unbeknownst historically,
Hoover was a humanitarian to so many,
and an engineer,
who thrived on organization.

Brings to mind some thoughts perhaps,
that Herbert Hoover had,
on the eve of the Great Depression;

Trying my heart out to succeed,
but more and more,
I find it rather impossible,
to help manage a system that has a mind of its own.
Such a mind needs some sort of control,
which evidently, I do not possess.

Maybe years from now,
people will say that at least I had good intentions.

1937 Ernest Hemingway

Ernest Hemingway was one of the greatest authors of the 20th Century. He had published seven novels, six short-story collections, and two nonfiction works. Among these were classics; *The Old Man and the Sea, For Whom the Bell Tolls, A Farwell to Arms, and The Sun Also Rises.* Hemingway was awarded the Nobel Prize in Literature in 1954.

Hemingway traveled extensively worldwide. As a journalist, he was stationed at many hot spots during the Spanish Civil War and World War II. During this time, he continued to write newspaper articles, novels, and short stories.

Sadly, Hemingway committed suicide on July 2, 1961, and his estate chose ghostwriters to complete his unpublished works. Three of his novels, four short-story collections, and three nonfiction works were published after his death.

Hemingway, the Bell Tolls for Thee

He had grown his beard longer than usual,
as the book he was writing in 1961,
was taking longer than anticipated.

He remembered writing, *A Farewell to Arms*,
about World War I, and writing news reports about,
being embroiled in a war on the beaches of Normandy,
and in so many war zones in Europe, and he wrote about
the liberation of Paris.
And before that, in 1937 through 1939,
where the fight for the Spanish state,
killed 500,000 of their own people.

And not very long before that,
he wrote, *The Sun also Rises* in 1926,
and then in 1937, *For Whom the Bell Tolls*
in response to that Spanish Civil War.

Finally, he wrote the last published book,
The Old Man and the Sea,
but he continued to write stories.

He was in so many war zones in Europe,
and he wrote of the liberation of Paris.

He had grown his beard longer than usual,
as the book and short stories were taking longer than anticipated.
He was writing about war and death,
and love and suffering,
and perhaps thinking before his suicide,
that the bell does toll for thee,
as he left so many books and stories unpublished,
for others to leave their imprint,
on war, death, and love and suffering.

1937 Nanking

In December of 1937, the Japanese Imperial Army marched into China's capital city of Nanking and proceeded to murder 300,000 out of 600,000 civilians and soldiers. The six weeks of carnage would become known as the Rape of Nanking.

The Nanking Massacre was a mass murder and war rape that occurred during the six weeks following the Japanese capture of Nanking, on December 13, 1937, during the Second Sino-Japanese War. In recent years the Japanese government has apologized for the deaths citing the casualties due to war. The Chinese government will not accept the apologies based on the war rationale. They believe the soldiers who perpetrated the murder and rape can not hide behind the war any longer.

Nanking

Chinese mothers, wives, daughters, sisters, aunts, grandmothers,
fathers, husbands, sons, brothers, uncles, grandfathers,
raped, murdered,
life's end.

Nanking immorality.
Crimes against humanity.
300,000 dead in 45 days,
6,660 dead every day.

The survivors watched,
the wretched soldiers,
under the cherry blossom trees,
so calm and contented.

Destruction came and went,
far and wide,
continued for years and years,
and eventually no one could hide
behind the war.

The day came,
when the flights of death
showed all people,
that whatever was done,
and all that they caused,
would tear them apart,
flesh off bones.

We, who just read the reports,
seem so far from it all,
and seem so small,
and years later,
a question arose,
can everyone hear the call,
for peace?

Peace was the message that needed to be fermented,
but we could only see,
the wretched soldiers
under the cherry blossom trees,
so calm and contented.

1937 Amelia

Amelia Earhart became the first woman to cross the Atlantic by airplane. After Amelia learned to fly, she desired to compete with men in all types of flying activities. One paramount goal was flying around the world and was a dream come true for Amelia.

Amelia set many flying records and championed the advancement of women in aviation. Also, she became the first person ever to fly solo from Hawaii to the U.S. mainland. On the trip flying around the world on July 2, 1937, her airplane disappeared. Her plane was never found and had officially declared lost at sea. Her disappearance remains one of the greatest mysteries of the twentieth century.

Amelia

A career that was a man's place in the paradigm.
She flew like an eagle and did it so well, if not better than a man.
She flew across the skies as long as possible before;

We don't know any more than that
because we lost track of her plane.

We know where she is now.
She's in the heavens,
floating above to show that being a woman,
where it used to be a man's place,
is not a constraint, but an advantage.

Women can now go where no other
women had gone before.

1932-1945 Eleanor Roosevelt

Anna Eleanor Roosevelt was an American political figure and diplomat. Interestingly, she was married to Franklin D. Roosevelt (FDR) in 1905, and was FDR's fifth cousin, and Theodore Roosevelt's niece. Eleanor served as the first lady of the United States from March 4, 1933, to April 12, 1945, during her husband's four terms in office. She became the longest-serving first lady of the United States.

Eleanor Roosevelt inspired many women to develop careers in areas that only men had explored. In 1946, after the death of FDR, Harry Truman, who became President, requested that Eleanor be a delegate to the newly formed United Nations. She was also an advocate for individuals with disabilities, and at the same time, became close friends with Helen Keller.

Eleanor

The first lady,
a human rights activist in a man's world.
Fighting for social and racial justice,
influenced women in a way never known before.
She was an activist for individuals with disabilities,
and a friend to Helen Keller.

Since Eleanor, politically, commercially, financially, and morally,
all women can aspire to be and do anything.

1941-1945 WWII

In some circles, World War II is the "last good war." The last good war label developed because America got involved in the war for good reasons: to stop Hitler's racist atrocities and prevent the spread of fascism. In WWII, the US military consisted of all individuals from all walks of life, coining the phrase "citizen soldiers." The fighting caused 60-80 million deaths worldwide, and the world was never the same again.

Post WW II shaped the world in the future in Europe and Asia. Japan developed as a United States ally, and countries in Western Europe grew into economic powerhouses with the help of the Marshall Plan. Russia and Eastern Europe became the Soviet Union and Iron Curtain countries. Eventually, General Dwight Eisenhower became the president of the United States in 1952.

The Last Good War

Giants among men:
Marshall, Eisenhower, Montgomery, Patton, and MacArthur.
Declaring victory before victory was had.
A driving force to inevitability.

The moment "we" hit that beach and took a step forward,
it was inevitable that we would win.
Days, months, years passed.
Taking back feet, yards, buildings, land,
cities, provinces, and countries,
from the despair of Nazism and Totalitarianism.

Then, finding out what kind of war was waged.
Finding death and cruelty beyond compare.
Besides the Great War killing an incomprehensible 37 million
civilians and military personel,
the Last Good War had its share of a doubly,
incomprehensible 60-80 million deaths.
The weapon's mobilizations.
Every facet of society had the same goal:
Winning the war.
What we accomplished in 3 ¾ years
we couldn't accomplish in the modern era.

Marshall, Eisenhower, Montgomery, Patton,
giants among men?
Because they were on top of our Fathers' - Grandfathers' and
Uncles' shoulders,
who were citizen soldiers,
fighting for what is right,
fighting the Last Good War.

1947 Roswell New Mexico

In July 1947, something happened near Roswell, New Mexico, during a severe thunderstorm. Was it a flying saucer? Was it a weather balloon? What happened?

The answer is nothing for many years until leading UFO researchers came across the story in the early 1980s and began the search for information and witnesses. That research brought them to Roswell, New Mexico looking for the public information officer who had been at Roswell Army Airfield in 1947. That officer was Lt. Walter Haut, and he still lived in Roswell. He remembered the press release and the orders from his commanding officer.

The military gathered the debris recovered by ranchers from the Roswell Army Airfield under the direction of base intelligence officer Major Jesse Marcel. On July 8, 1947, public information officer Lt. Walter Haut issued a press release under orders from base commander Col. William Blanchard, "that we have in our possession a flying saucer."

The next day, another press release was issued, this time from Gen. Roger Ramey, stating it was a weather balloon. That was the start of the best-known and well-documented UFO coverup.

Unidentified, Maybe

Unidentified Flying Objects,
were identified at first.
A craft and evidence of language symbols,
quickly taken back,
then identified as a weather balloon in 1947.

Decades of reporting,
dealing with UFOs,
and now Unidentified Aerial Phenomena (UAPs).
Now, the Navy agreeing to publish accounts,
of different shapes in the sky,
to and from the water.

Finally, we thought
disclosure about UFOs, UAPs, and government activity
would be a reality.

Disclosure was not going well,
with the 9-page report in 2021.

134 sightings were evaluated.
133 could not be further evaluated.
1 was identified.
Eerily, strangely, ironically,
as a weather balloon in 2021.

1953 Edmund Hilary and Mt. Everest

In 1953, Edmond Hilary of New Zealand became the first man to reach the summit of Mt. Everest. Hillary had climbed many mountain tops and made the Mt. Everest climb many times before he could conquer the summit.

The Hill

I thought I knew,
      all there was to know.
Then I started up the hill,
climbing, climbing,
         so very hard,
to find that which is so scarce.

It seems that's the way it is,
everything that we ever want,
           or can't have,
always at the top of a hill.
  Just steep enough,
      to make us stop.

But when climbing, climbing,
      has not gotten you there,
think of what seems to be at the top.
      Not a pot of gold,
but more of yourself.

1955 Rosa Parks

Rosa Parks was an American activist in the civil rights movement best known for her crucial role in the Montgomery bus boycott. Rosa refused to go to the back of the bus. The United States Congress has called her "the first lady of civil rights," and "the mother of the freedom movement."

Rosa

She didn't take the back seat,
to any man or woman.
She and Martin,
what a movement.
Towards the force of equality,
the force of justice,
the force of equal opportunity.

Rosa was the "common woman, and man".
The woman who raised her children
who had to face discrimination,
faced discrimination herself.

But somehow the discriminating police officer,
arresting her for trying to sit up at the front of the bus,
seemed to realize that the historic moment was,
upon all of us at that time,
when Rosa was paving the way for
equality for women and men alike.

1955-1975 War in Vietnam

In 1964 and 1965, the U.S. became involved in what was named the second Indo-China war. To Americans, it was the War in Vietnam. From 1963-1968 the U.S. ramped up to full strength and would remain in Vietnam for over ten years The U.S. fought the war from 1964 through 1975, and the lives of more than 56,000 troops were lost.

The War in Vietnam was subjected to protests in the U.S., lobbying for the war's end. The Paris peace talks of 1974 through 1975 resulted in the U.S. withdrawing all troops and airlifting essential South Vietnamese citizens. This airlift featured the famous photograph of that final helicopter perched on a rooftop with women and children appearing to ascend into the heavens.

Due to politics, the drug trade, and the military-industrial complex, the war in Vietnam was known in the annals of U.S. history books as the unwinable war.

Vietnam

They called it the French Indochina War in '55,
and the U.S. inherited the battle in '63 through '75.
Eventually it was the "War in Vietnam,"
back in the day politics, drug trade,
the military industrial complex,
turned into the unwinable war.

56,000 lives lost of our youngest and,
many of our most vulnerable,
due to class and race.

Carpet bombing and defoliant spraying Agent Orange,
body counts on the nightly news.
Thousands of Vietnamese killed each week,
but under reporting U.S. deaths each day.

Some of the young people who didn't go to war,
demonstrated for peace,
and after an insane series of disagreements
on the shape of the table,
the Paris peace talks started at a round table,
and ended with scenes of that helicopter
and South Vietnamese women and children,
climbing aboard as it appeared to ascend into the heavens.

1960-2021 Jane Goodall

Jane Goodall is an English primatologist and anthropologist most known for her work with chimpanzees. She lived in Africa for many years, getting closer and closer to these chimps. They then appeared to accept her as their own.

Considered to be the world's foremost expert on chimpanzees, Goodall is best known for her 60-year study of social and family interactions of wild chimpanzees in Gombe Stream National Park in Tanzania starting in 1960. She witnessed human-like behaviors amongst chimpanzees, including armed conflict. Jane does return frequently.

Jane

Primatologist, anthropologist, her chimpanzees,
communicating to her,
through touch and feeling the energy.

These chimps speak to her.
Her warmth is electric.
Her presence felt like all humanity.
She could speak to them.

Perhaps these are Jane Goodall's feelings
on working with her chimps.
They seemed to feel the same about her.

1960 U2 and Gary Powers

During the early 1960s, the U.S. conducted reconnaissance flights over the Soviet Union airspace using the U2 spy plane. The plane had no weapons on board, only cameras.

The primary mission of the U-2s was overflying the Soviet Union. Soviet intelligence had been aware of encroaching U-2 flights at least since 1958, if not earlier. We knew the Soviets had missiles with nuclear warheads, but of course, we had to confirm this information. Then, in 1960, the Soviet military shot down one of the U.S. U2 spy planes. The U.S. pilot was Gary Francis Powers.

The Soviet Union decided to make an example out of Powers and threatened to execute him. A trade was then implemented for a Soviet spy in return for Powers.

What We Already Knew

We could see all the Soviet Union with one flight.
We needed to know our cold war enemy.

Considering his last name,
he was less than powerless.
He flew the embattled U2 spy plane,
which carried no weapons,
to show that we meant no harm,
but was accused of being a spy,
and traded away for another spy.

All of this, trying to prove to the United Nations what we
already knew.

1963 JFK

John Fitzgerald Kennedy (1917 – 1963), referred to by his initials JFK, or by his nickname, Jack, served as the 35th president of the United States from 1961 until his assassination on November 22, 1963. JFK's administration managed situations in the Soviet Union, Cuba, Latin America, and the Apollo space program to land a man on the Moon. He also supported the civil rights movement.

On November 22, 1963, the assassination of JFK occurred in Dallas, Texas, and Vice President Lyndon Johnson assumed the presidency upon Kennedy's death. According to the Warren Commission, Lee Harvey Oswald was arrested for the crime. The FBI and the Warren Commission concluded Oswald had acted alone in the assassination, but Jack Ruby shot and killed Oswald two days later. Various groups contested the Warren Report and believed that Kennedy was the victim of a conspiracy. Many believe JFK could have been assassinated by organized crime, Fidel Castro, other individuals, and even Lyndon Johnson. These conspiracy theories were never proven. After Kennedy's death, Congress enacted many of his proposals, including the Civil Rights Act, and the Revenue Act of 1964.

JFK

He was a man of the people.
President of the people, for the people, by the people.
Peace Corps, Latin American progress, Civil Rights Movement,
all in less than 3 years.
So much promise.

His election was closer than anyone thought
or anyone thinks now.
Many people are needed to get elected,
but a lot in return is needed.

Deals were made,
and some promises kept
for any number of things.

Even though Jack was a man of the people,
when you make deals with multiple devils,
which one will end in
breaking the promise?

1968 RFK

Robert Kennedy (1925-1968), referred to by his initials RFK or by his nickname Bobby, was the brother of President John F. Kennedy. RFK was an American lawyer and politician who served as the 64th United States Attorney General from January 1961 to September 1964, and as a U.S. Senator from New York from January 1965 until his assassination on June 6, 1968.

Before being Attorney General, RFK served on many legal committees, including those investigating organized crime. Conspiracy theories in the JFK assassination include speculation that organized crime killed JFK so that Bobby would not be Attorney General any longer and could not continue pursuing organized crime.

There was also a snake metaphor depicting JFK as the snake's head and RFK as the snake's body. Without the head of the snake, the body of the snake will die.

RFK

Bobby was a man of the people.
Attorney, politician, committee member,
Attorney General, Presidential candidate.

The mob said he was the body of the snake,
but had to be dealt with
no matter the end result
of his candidacy.

The head of the snake, JFK,
was dealt with in '63,
and then the body would die without its head..

Bobby was a man of the people,
explaining to followers of Martin,
that a white man also had killed his brother.
Eerily and strangely he was assassinated,
within three months of Martin's assassination,
and in '68, within 5 years of his brother's.

1968 MLK

Martin Luther King Jr. (1929-1968) was an American Baptist minister and activist who became the American civil rights movement leader from 1955 until his assassination in 1968. Popular culture listed "Martin" as his nickname. King advanced civil rights through nonviolence and civil disobedience. He was the son of early civil rights activist, Martin Luther King Sr.

MLK participated in and led marches for black's right to vote, desegregation, labor rights, and other fundamental civil rights. King led the 1955 Montgomery Bus Boycott, and later became the Southern Christian Leadership Conference (SCLC) president. He led the unsuccessful Albany Movement in Albany, Georgia, but he helped organize nonviolent 1963 protests in Birmingham, Alabama. Martin helped organize the 1963 March on Washington, where he delivered his famous "I Have a Dream" speech on the steps of the Lincoln Memorial.

Martin Luther King Jr.

Martin was a man of the people, and a man of God.
Racial activist, advocated nonviolence, civil disobedience,
and also was assassinated;
after Jack and before Bobby.

Coincidently, Bobby and Martin
were both killed within 5 years of JFK.

Conspiracy theories abound,
but many of us feel
that we know the truth.

9/11/2001 Tuesday

On September 11, 2001, militants associated with the terrorist group al Qaeda hijacked four airliners and carried out suicide attacks against the United States. Terrorists flew two of the airliners into the twin towers of the World Trade Center in NYC, a third plane hit the Pentagon just outside Washington, D.C., and the fourth plane crashed in a field in Shanksville, Pennsylvania, after some of the passengers disarmed the terrorists stating, "let's roll."

Almost 3,000 people died during the 9/11 terrorist attacks, which triggered major U.S. initiatives to combat terrorism and defined the presidency of George W. Bush.

Nine-Eleven

Many stories that I read in the newspapers have never directly involved my life,
as most people who live in the suburbs and commute to the city, or live in the city that never sleeps,
who go along with their lives, working, loving, learning, thinking, shopping,
eating, laughing, caring, and on and on and on,
never expecting that any of these stories would directly involve their lives.

That Tuesday, the second week in September,
a week after my twenty-fourth wedding anniversary,
when my wife was dying, my kids were in college, in high school, and in
middle school, when we were watching TV and having coffee,
much like I am sure, so many of us.

Tuesday morning news footage,
those planes, flying into those Twin Towers, our Pentagon,
obliterating, vaporizing, almost 3,000 bodies, but not their souls.

Those towers, became my towers over the years,
visiting so many times, to see my customers, to see my old boss,
my Dutch uncle, my mentor in a key time in my life, after surgery, after
questioning my ability, who said it like it was, who called on September 9th,
to see how my wife was feeling, and giving me support.
Who I think about all the time, feeling his presence, when déjà vu in business
happens.

That Tuesday, when our lives changed, my children's lives changed, to sober
us into realizing that, in an instant, the enemy from within, can become the
enemy from without.

As our world and "they" and "those" people and "it," can change to affect my
world: my life ultimately, specifically, internally, and externally.

That day, that Tuesday the second week in September, my day of heartache,
for sorrow, for all those families, for those 3,000 souls,
when we lost even more than mothers, fathers, brothers, a mentor, a friend,
a Dutch uncle.

We lost part of our past, our future, our friendship,
and our own safety,
as we go along with our lives, working, weaving in and out on the highway,
walking on the sidewalk, loving, learning, thinking, chatting, shopping,
eating, laughing, caring,

And of not knowing;
if it could happen again, when we all least expect it.

2011 Tsunami in Myagi Prefecture

The 2011 Tsunami, caused by an underwater earthquake, in Asia, specifically in Japan, was a horrible storm system that had devastated the shores of Japan and many of the cities and counties called Prefectures. The Tsunami caused the death of thousands of Japanese and thousands of other lives in Asia. Ishinomaki, is the city with the most casualties numbering over 3,900.

The official figures in Japan released in 2021 reported 19,747 deaths, 6,242 injured, and 2,556 people were missing. A report from 2015 indicated 228,863 people still living away from their homes in either temporary housing or due to permanent relocation.

Tsunami in Ishinomaki, Myagi Prefecture

Fishing down by the shore,
in Ishinomaki,
in the Myagi prefecture,
with my 3 children and wife,
the joys in my life.

When, what felt like a millisecond later,
came the sirens;
I heard about the sirens,
but never actually heard them before.

I gathered my children,
and screamed to my wife.
In what felt like a millisecond,
came the waves,
swallowing up my wife,
and everything about her life,
and about our lives.

And over 3900 other lives.

Managing to swoop up my son and 2 daughters,
but watching all our possessions floating away.

Then the children and I could only
sit down by the shore,
in Ishinomaki,
in the Myagi prefecture,
and cry.

2013 Boston Marathon Bombing

During the annual Boston Marathon on April 15, 2013 (Patriots Day 2013), two terrorists planted two bombs, which detonated 210 yards apart at roughly the same time, near the finish line of the race, killing three people and injuring hundreds of others, including 17 who lost limbs.

It was a horrible scene, and those who lost limbs battled back to run again on future Patriot Days.

Boston Oh Boston

Boston, oh Boston,
the sages call out in despair.
What have they done to our city?
Boston oh Boston,
what the British were unable to do,
could these terrorists do?
We think not!

So many before,
have given their lives,
in defense of liberty, a free land,
are swirling around in the heavens,
holding their hands,
saying
Boston, oh Boston,
don't despair.

The sons of liberty will defend you,
the marathoners will run,
again and again on Patriot's Day.

Whether in heartbreak in the name of the fallen,
or in sadness and shock,
without the limbs they started on Patriots' Day 2013,
but with their new limbs,
they will walk again,
they will run again,
they will live again!

Boston oh Boston,
don't despair,
a new day will come,
when the sages will say,
"They have not destroyed our city,"

but made everyone more aware,
that Freedom is not Free.

2016-2020 Politics

November 2020, marked the 59th presidential election in the United States. These times are unprecedented. Indeed, these events have been and undoubtedly will continue to affect all of us. All issues have become contentious, and some raise serious questions about the American political order.

The Pandemic, vaccinations, masks or no masks, the Supreme Court, immigration, racism, climate change, and election forecasting all play a part in 21st-century politics.

Politics of the 21st century

History of our nation,
speaks to us about patriotism,
fighting in wars, standing up for a cause,
greater than oneself.

Instead, there is the Trojan Horse,
of wrapping oneself
in the American Flag,
the militia flag,
and even the confederate flag.

What should we make of this?
How do we move forward?

We reconcile differences.
Work in teams.
Work against crime.
Work for the masses.
Work for the public health.
We reconcile differences.

With as much strength as we can muster,
we are dedicated to doing the right thing.

1945-2021 History

1945 through 2021 represents the history of Baby Boomers. The parent's lives of baby boomers are also part of boomer's history. There have been some key events and key dates that represent so much. History has had an indelible effect on the psyche. So many boomers can remember precisely where they were when the JFK assassination took place. Octogenarians could remember where they were when VE and VJ days occurred in 1945, and Generation Xs can remember where they were when 9/11 happened. Now the Covid-19 Pandemic will be a focal point to the current youth.

Try to live by the edict: remember history lest we are doomed to repeat it.

I Remember Everything

I remember everything.
I remember the JFK assassination in '63,
and the RFK Assassination in '68 and the MLK Assassination in '68,
and the feeling as a 14-year-old that a conspiracy was true.

I remember everything.

I remember my father telling me about the great depression,
and the bread lines,
and World War II,
and his working on sea planes 18 hours a day,
'42 thru '45.

I remember everything.

I remember stories about my grandfather,
telling me about the piece work he did at the Brooklyn Navy yard,
polishing brass fittings for two cents a fitting in 1914-1915,
and his service in the signal corps during WW I, using pigeons.
Followed up using pigeons to communicate to friends in Florida.

I remember everything.

I remember when Harry Truman died,
and I remember an announcement by the high school principal,
that a classmate's brother died in Vietnam.

I remember everything.

I remember learning about segregation and Brown vs the Board of
Education,
and George Wallace blocking children and entrances to schools in
Alabama.
I remember a guidance counselor in junior high school telling me,
that I would never go to college,
and I thought about that every time as a I earned my
Associates degree,
and my Bachelor's degree,
and my MBA,
and will remember that when I complete my Doctorate.

I remember everything.

I remember Watergate,
Nixon's enemies list,
and the start of dirty tricks in politics.

I remember everything.

I remember the space program,
and the Mercury flights,
and the Gemini flights,
and the early Apollo flights.

I remember everything.

I remember Apollo 8 and
Frank Borman' Christmas Eve broadcast from Lunar orbit,
and Apollo 11,
the '69 landing on the moon,
and all the missions after that, also landing on the moon.
I also remember the public not being interested anymore,
except for me and my son.

I remember everything.

I remember the 6-day war in '67,
and when Israel defeated five Arab nations,
and it was declared a modern-day miracle,
when Jewish children of 13 needed to see an actual miracle,
like shown in the Five Books of Moses..

I remember everything.

I remember '68,
and the Czech revolt
and the tanks on TV,
and the Polish uprising,
and the Solidarity movement of the 80s.

I remember everything.

I remember the fall of communism,
And the Berlin Wall coming down.,
And peace arriving in Eastern Europe.

I remember everything.

I'll be at peace and hopeful,
That my children and grandchildren will always remember,
All I've told them,
about all the Poetry in History.

BIBLIOGRAPHY

Page   **Reference**

10   https://www.britannica.com/event/Crusades
https://www.quora.com/How-did-the-Ottoman-Empire-change-after-WWI
https://www.fbi.gov/investigate/wmd/major-cases

12   Jehanne Darc (Pernoud Clin 1998, pp. 220–221)

14   Swenson, Kristine (2006). Medical Women and Victorian Fiction, University of Missouri Press

16   https://www.battlefields.org/learn/civil-war/battles/gettysburg

18   https://immigrationhistory.org/timeline/

20   https://www.britannica.com/biography/John-J-Pershing

22   "The Wright Brothers and the invention of the aerial age". National Air & Space Museum. Smithsonian Institution. Archived from the original on 13 August 2015. Retrieved 21 September 2010.

24   https://www.cdc.gov/flu/pandemic-resources/1918-pandemic-h1n1.html

26   Bondyopadhyay, P.K. (1998). "Sir J.C. Bose diode detector received Marconi's first transatlantic wireless signal of December 1901 (the 'Italian Navy Coherer' Scandal Revisited)". Proceedings of the IEEE. 86: 259. doi:10.1109/5.65877

28   "Armistice: The End of World War I, 1918". Eyewitness to History. Archived from the original on 26 November 2018. Retrieved 26 November 2018.

30   Goldsmith, B., (2005). Obsessive Genius: The Inner World of Marie Curie

32   https://www.history.com/topics/great-depression
https://hoover.archives.gov/

34   "Hemingway on War and Its Aftermath". archives.gov. August 15, 2016. Retrieved July 11, 2017

36   https://www.crf-usa.org/bill-of-rights-in-action/bria-18-3-b-the-rape-of-nanking

     historyplace.com/worldhistory/genocide/nanking.htm

38   Amelia Earhart NOV 9, 2009 History.com editors

40   Moore, Frazier (September 10, 2014) PBS "The Roosevelts, Associate Press. Archived from on September 10, 2014

42   https://www.britannica.com/event/World-War-II

44   The International UFO Museum & Research Center, 114 N Main Street. Rosewell, NM

46   "Edmund Hillary". New Zealand History. Wellington, New Zealand: Research and Publishing Group of the New Zealand Ministry for Culture and Heritage. Retrieved 15 February 2018.

BIBLIOGRAPHY

Page   **Reference**

48 "An Act of Courage, The Arrest Records of Rosa Parks". National Archives. August 15, 2015. Retrieved December 1, 2020.

50 Factasy. "The Vietnam War or Second Indochina War". PRLog. Retrieved 29 June 2013

52 Holloway, M., (1997). Profile: Jane Goodall- Gombe's Famous Primates; Scientific American

54 http://garypowers.com/wp-content/uploads/2018/12/fgp-bg-img-w1920-v2.jpg

56 https://www.archives.gov/research/jfk

58 Jackman,T.(2018)Who killed Bobby Kennedy? His son RFK Jr. doesn't believe it was Sirhan Sirhan Washington Post.

60 Jackman, T. (2018) Who killed Martin Luther King Jr.? His family believes James Earl Ray was framed. Washington Post.

62 https://www.911memorial.org/911-faqs

64 Branigan, T. (2011). Tsunami, earthquake, nuclear crisis-now Japan faces power cuts. The Guardian. Retrieved 2011

68 Kotz,D. (2013). "Injury toll from Marathon bombs reduced to 264". The Boston Globe. Archived from the original on March 31, 2019. Retrieved April 29, 2013.

70 hbr.org/amp/2020/07/fixing-u-s-politics

PHOTO SOURCES AND LINKS

Page   **Reference**

Cover Eisenhower - https://www.kshs.org/km/items/view/210892

Cover Jane Goodall - https://photos.com/featured/jane-goodall-with-a-chimpanzee-bettmann.html

Cover Wright Bros. - https://www.biography.com/video/5-facts-about-the-wright-brothers-434030147654

Cover Amelia Earhart https://www.nbcnews.com/news/world/search-still-amelia-earhart-80-years-after-she-disappeared-n778291

Cover Marie Curie - https://www.atomicarchive.com/resources/biographies/marie-curie.html

Cover Marconi Front https://www.mentalfloss.com/article/558104/facts-about-guglielmo-marconi

Cover Martin Luther King - https://www.theatlantic.com/photo/2015/01/remembering-martin-luther-king-jr-in-photos/384635/

Cover Spanish Flu https://commons.wikimedia.org/wiki/File:Camp_Funston,_at_Fort_Riley,_Kansas,_during_the_1918_Spanish_flu_pandemic.jpg

Cover Typewriter - https://www.crushpixel.com/stock-photo/old typewriter-1551693.html

10   https://commons.wikimedia.org/wiki/File:People%27s_Crusade_(cs).JPG
     https://commons.wikimedia.org/wiki/File:Map_of_US_Murder_Rate.svg

12   https://commons.wikimedia.org/wiki/File:Personal_Recollections_of_Joan_of_Arc,_1896,_Figure_29.jpg

14   https://commons.wikimedia.org/wiki/File:Florence_Nightingale._Photograph_by_Millbourn._Wellcome_V0026906.jpg

16   https://commons.wikimedia.org/wiki/File:Pennsylvania,_Gettysburg._A_Harvest_of_Death_-_NARA_-_533310.tif

18   https://commons.wikimedia.org/wiki/File:Ellis_island_1902.jpg

20   https://commons.wikimedia.org/wiki/File:Gen._J.J._Pershing_LCCN2014701072.jpg

22   https://commons.wikimedia.org/wiki/File:1902_Wright_Brothers%27_Glider_Tests_-_GPN-2002-000125.jpg

24   https://commons.wikimedia.org/wiki/File:Emergency_hospital_during_Influenza_epidemic,_Camp_Funston,_Kansas_-_NCP_1603.jpg

26   https://commons.wikimedia.org/wiki/File:Marconi_Type_106_crystal_radio_receiver.jpg
     https://commons.wikimedia.org/wiki/File:Leonard_Marconi.jpg

PHOTO SOURCES AND LINKS

Page   **Reference**

28   https://commons.wikimedia.org/wiki/File:New_Zealand_troops_in_the_
trenches,_World_War_I.jpg

30   https://commons.wikimedia.org/wiki/File:Marie-Curie.jp

32   https://commons.wikimedia.org/wiki/File:HerbertHoover
https://commons.wikimedia.org/wiki/File:Depression,_Breadlines-

34   https://commons.wikimedia.org/wiki/File:Ernest_Hemingway_Aboard_the_
Pilar_1935.png

36   https://commons.wikimedia.org/wiki/File:Nanking_Massacre_victims.jpg

38   https://commons.wikimedia.org/wiki/File:Pilote_Amelia_Earhart_-_Pilot_
Amelia_Earhart_-_Flickr_-_Nationaal_Archief.jpg

40   https://commons.wikimedia.org/wiki/File:Eleanor_Roosevelt_portrait_1933.jpg

42   https://commons.wikimedia.org/wiki/File:General_Dwight_D._Eisenhower_
meeting_the_troops_prior_to_the_Normandy_invasion.tif

44   https://commons.wikimedia.org/wiki/File:RoswellDailyRecordJuly8,1947.jpg

46   https://commons.wikimedia.org/wiki/File:Edmund_Hillary,_c._1953,_
autograph_removed.jpg

https://commons.wikimedia.org/wiki/File:Everest_North_Face_toward_
Base_Camp_Tibet_Luca_Galuzzi_2006.jpg

48   https://commons.wikimedia.org/wiki/File:Rosa_Parks_being_
fingerprinted_by_Deputy_Sheriff_D.H._Lackey_after_being_arrested_on_
February_22,_1956,_during_the_Montgomery_bus_boycott.jpg

50   https://commons.wikimedia.org/wiki/File:US-Army-troops-taking-break-
while-on-patrol-in-Vietnam-War.jpg'

https://commons.wikimedia.org/wiki/File:Evacuees_from_Vietnam_04_on_
USS_Midway_(CVA-41)_in_1975.jpg

52   https://commons.wikimedia.org/wiki/File:Johanna_lohr_jane-goodall.jpg

https://commons.wikimedia.org/wiki/File:2006-12-09_Chipanzees_D_
Bruyere.JPG

54   http://garypowers.com/wp-content/uploads/2018/12/fgp-bg-img-w1920-v2.jpg

56   https://commons.wikimedia.org/wiki/File:John_F._Kennedy_-_NARA_-
_518134.jpg

58   https://commons.wikimedia.org/wiki/File:Kennedy_1968_(a).jpg

60   https://commons.wikimedia.org/wiki/File:Martin_Luther_King,_Jr..jpg

62   https://commons.wikimedia.org/wiki/File:Collection-of-unattributed-
photographs-of-the-september-11th-terrorist-attack-52.jpg

PHOTO SOURCES AND LINKS

Page   **Reference**

64   https://commons.wikimedia.org/wiki/File:Damage_from_the_tsunami_
     inundation_of_Kamaishi_city_with_a_maximum_runup_height_
     of_11.7_m_-1-6-2011-_and_of_Ofunato_city_with_a_maximum_runup_
     height_of_10

66   https://commons.wikimedia.org/wiki/File:Boston_Marathon_explosions_
     (8653924130).jpg

68   https://commons.wikimedia.org/wiki/File:United_States_Capitol_Building.jpg

70   https://commons.wikimedia.org/wiki/File:NYC_Collage_3.jpg